· Let's Make ·
ANIMATED FLIP BOOKS

David Hurtado

This library edition published in 2023 by Walter Foster Jr.,
an imprint of The Quarto Group
100 Cummings Center, Suite 265D
Beverly, MA 01915, USA.

© 2023 Quarto Publishing Group USA Inc.
Artwork © 2016 David Hurtado

Distributed in the United States and Canada by
Lerner Publisher Services
241 First Avenue North
Minneapolis, MN 55401 U.S.A.
www.lernerbooks.com

First Library Edition

Library of Congress Cataloging-in-Publication Data

Names: Hurtado, David, author.
Title: Let's make animated flip books / David Hurtado.
Other titles: Flipping out
Description: First Library Edition. | Beverly, MA : Walter Foster Jr.,
   2023. | Audience: Ages 8+ | Audience: Grades 4-6
Identifiers: LCCN 2022019964 | ISBN 9780760380871 (library binding)
Subjects: LCSH: Flip books--Juvenile literature.
Classification: LCC NC1764.85 .H87 2023 | DDC 741.5/8--dc23/eng/20220714
LC record available at https://lccn.loc.gov/2022019964

Printed in USA
10 9 8 7 6 5 4 3 2 1

TABLE OF CONTENTS

INTRODUCTION 4
    Do It Yourself 5
    Tools and Materials 6

CHAPTER 1: THE BASICS OF ANIMATION 8
    Animating a Stick Figure 9
    Dynamics: Animating a Ball 12
    Timing 16

CHAPTER 2: SIMPLE MOVEMENTS 20
    Keyframes and Inbetweens 21
    Walk Cycles, Run Cycles, and Jumps 24
    Anticipation 28

CHAPTER 3: CHARACTER DESIGN 30
    Your Artistic Freedom 31
    Facial Expressions 36
    Animating a Face 38

CHAPTER 4: WRITING A STORY 40
    Keeping It Simple 41
    Storyboarding 42
    Animating a Flying Superhero 44
    Dr. Jekyll and Mr. Hyde 50

CHAPTER 5: TAKING IT TO THE NEXT LEVEL 56
    Animating Dancers 57
    Animating Animals 60
    Binding a Flip Book 62

ABOUT THE AUTHOR 64

INTRODUCTION

A flip book consists of a series of static pictures that change only slightly from page to page. Holding the book in one hand, you use the thumb of your other hand to flip through the pages quickly, making the pictures appear to move. They don't actually move, of course, but your eyes and brain tell you that they do!

Animated flip books show motion, like a bird's wings flapping.

DO IT YOURSELF

This book will show you how to create a flip book from start to finish. Start by following the instructions provided here, but don't be afraid to branch out and create your own plots, animations, and designs. Creativity will be your best asset!

TOOLS AND MATERIALS

You don't need to spend a lot of money on supplies to make animated flip books—all you really need are a pencil and notepad. However, you can enhance your animation skills and make your flip book look even more amazing using the basic materials listed here!

Pencils
A standard HB pencil (or No. 2 pencil) works well for doodling and shading. Use H (hard) pencils for lighter marks and B (soft) pencils for darker, more vigorous strokes or motion effects.

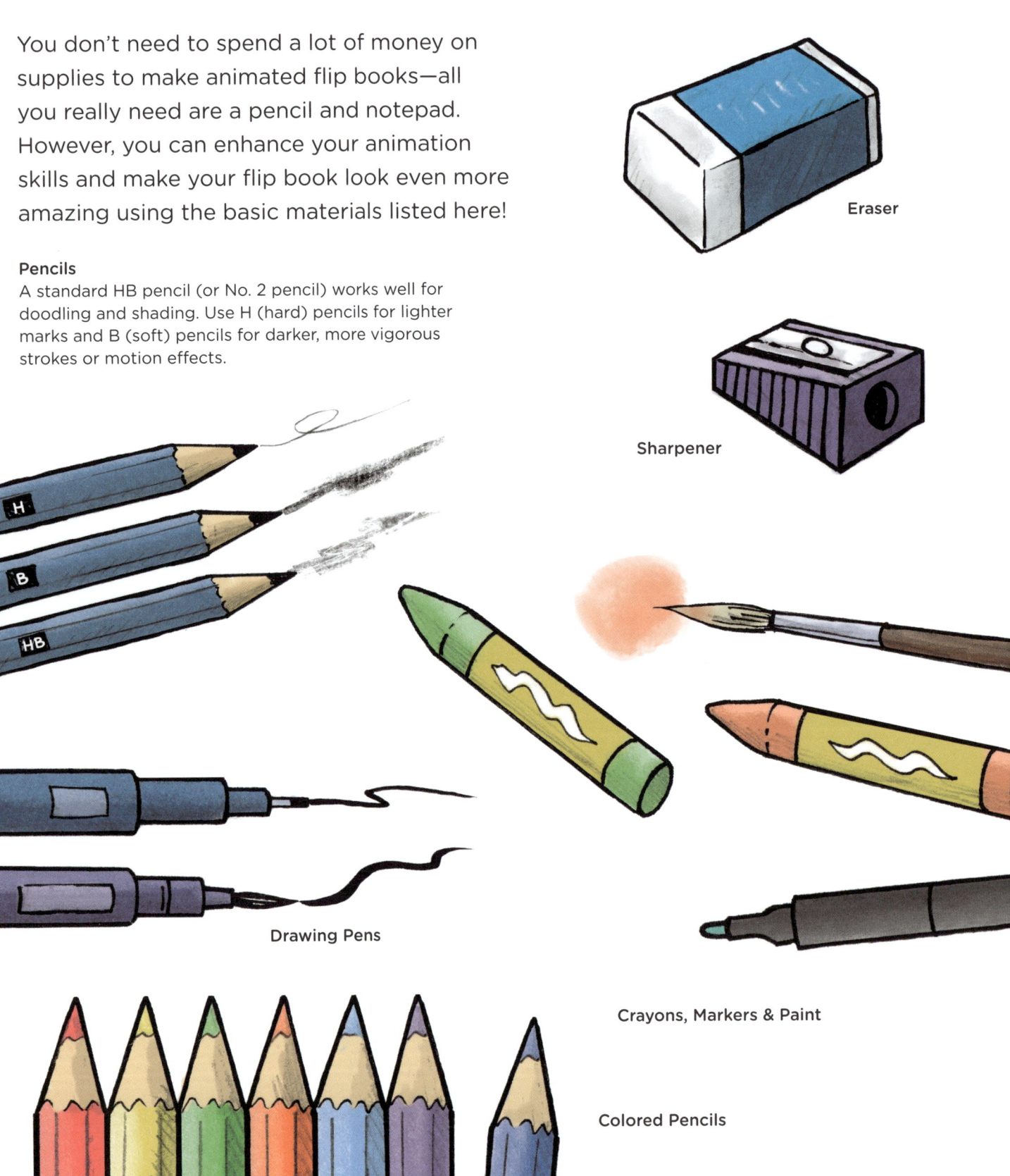

Eraser

Sharpener

Drawing Pens

Crayons, Markers & Paint

Colored Pencils

Paper & Notepads
Do a quick, careful test of the paper or notepad before purchasing to make sure the pages flip well. For simple flip book animations, memo blocks and small notebooks work best.

Binder Clips
Binder clips provide a simple way to bind and test your flip books.

Stapler

Scissors

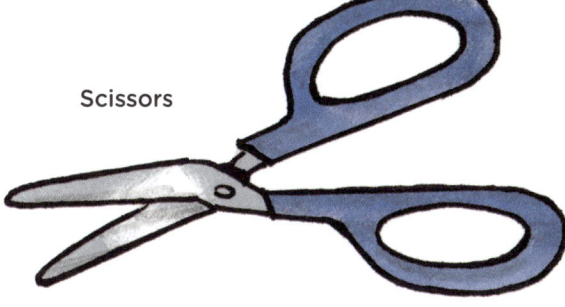

Ruler & Triangles

Light Box

A light box will help you trace over your previous drawings—an invaluable tool for advanced flip book artists!

CHAPTER ONE

THE BASICS OF ANIMATION

ANIMATING A STICK FIGURE

Creating a stick figure for a flip book teaches you the principles of hand-drawn animation in a simple and enjoyable way. In this exercise, you will create basic stories; design characters; and draw keyframes, inbetweens, and walk cycles.

This exercise has a very simple plot: A man jumps so high on a diving board that it springs him into space! The main character's design is also quite straightforward: a simple stick man with black shorts and crazy hair. Each picture in this project has a description of the scene and the timing, or the number of pages it will take to animate it.

Bathers are taking a dip in a swimming pool on a hot summer's day. You will need to draw the same picture for about 12 pages to establish the shot.

The main character enters the scene and walks to the diving board. This will run for about 15 to 20 pages of your flip book. Alternate the positions of the character's legs and arms on each page.

The stick figure main character stands on the diving board and raises his arms. Repeat this picture 8 times to create a pause.

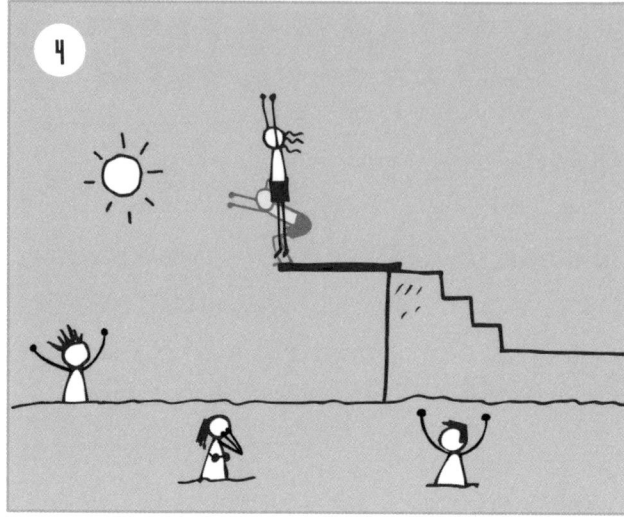

The stick figure raises his arms and stretches his legs. The first action will take 2 pages, and the stretching another 2.

He bounces downward, preparing to jump. This will take 2 pages.

He jumps up, but it's not a big jump at first. This jump will take 2 pages.

He bounces down, and the diving board stretches. Use 6 pages to illustrate from the top of the previous jump until the landing on the diving board.

The jump is too high, and the character springs off the scene. This action will take 3 or 4 pages.

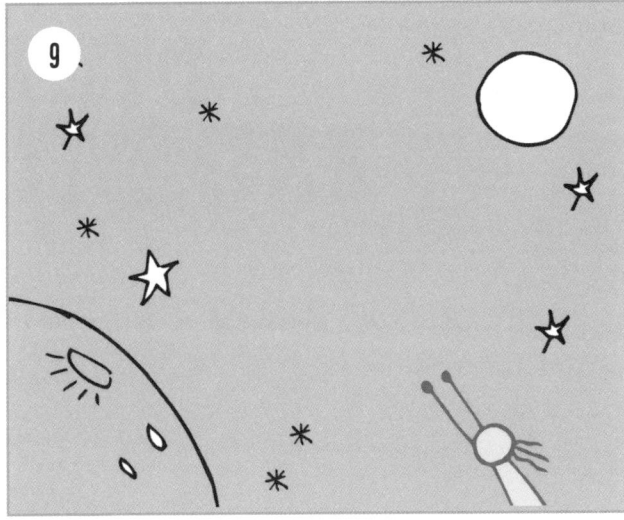

Establish a shot in space. Your stick figure will enter the scene at the lower right corner. Draw the empty space picture for 6 pages.

Draw the stick figure's trajectory from the lower right corner to the upper right corner over 12 pages.

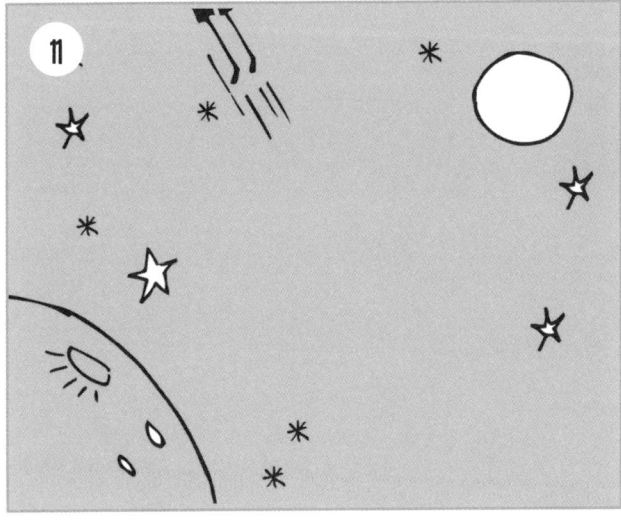

The stick figure is now out of the scene. Draw the empty space picture for at least 6 pages.

The end credits appear for 6 pages.

DYNAMICS: ANIMATING A BALL

Animating a ball is often one of the very first things that a beginning animator like you will learn. It might even be your first experience with certain important animation concepts such as timing, spacing, gravity, and weight.

FROM A TO B

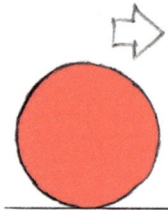 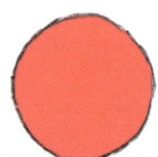

The goal here is to move a ball from point A to point B. This movement will happen over six pages.

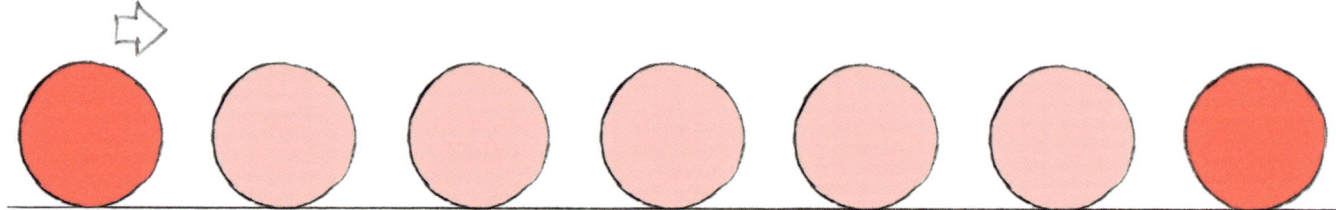

On the first page, draw a horizontal line across the page and a circle on the left side of the line. Trace the same line over the next five pages. On the sixth page, draw a circle on the right side of the line.

Using the sequence above as a guideline, draw circles on the pages in between, changing the circles' positions slightly on each page. Flip through your flip book to test your animation, and notice how the ball moves.

TIP
Motion is not always uniform. Sometimes an animated object can start slowly only to accelerate later. The opposite can also happen. Varying the spacing in an animation will change the speed of motion.

VARYING SPEED

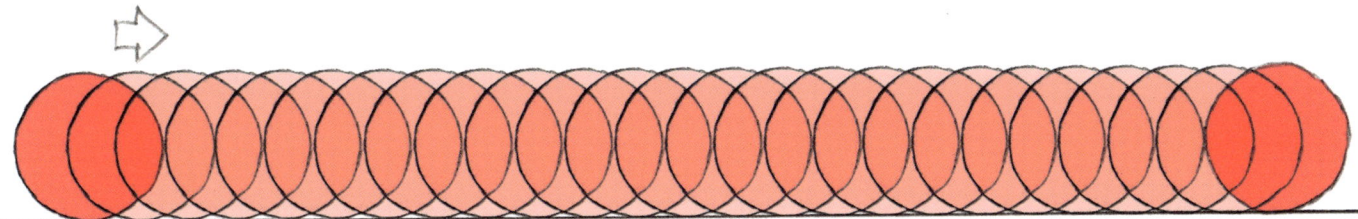

Now let's repeat the same exercise, making the ball move slower this time. On the first page of a flip book or notepad, draw a horizontal line and a circle on the left side of the line. Trace the same line on 25 pages. On page 25, draw the circle at point B.

Then draw the circle on each of the rest of the pages, changing its position slightly on each page. Test your animation, and notice that it takes about 1 second for the ball to move across the line. (The timing will vary slightly.)

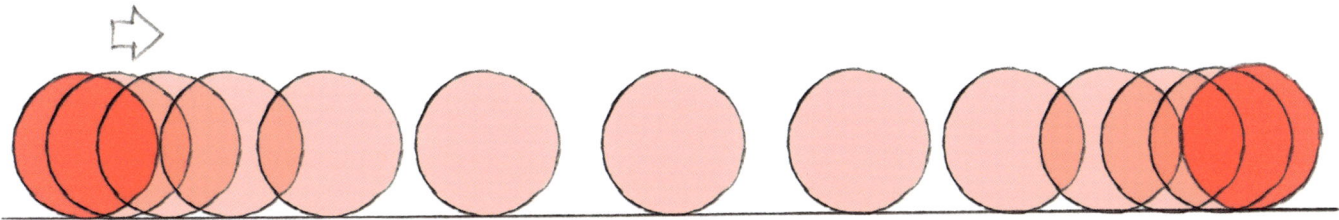

Now vary the circles' positions so they're more spaced out in the center. This changes the animation's spacing and varies the ball's speed.

BOUNCING BALL

Another classic animation exercise, illustrating a bouncing ball will teach you about gravity and weight. You can achieve the illusion of gravitational force by changing the spacing in your animations as well as by squashing and stretching the subject.

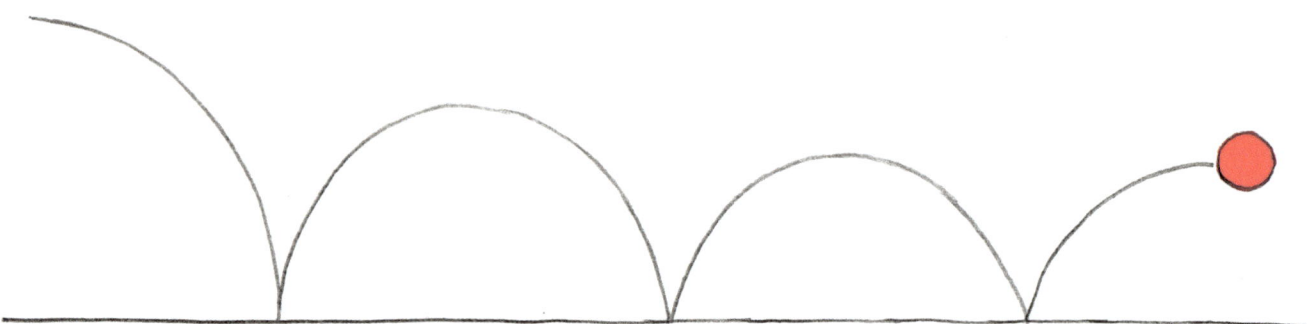

You will need 32 blank pages in a flip book or notepad for this exercise. On the first page, draw a horizontal line to represent the ground. Then draw a motion line. This motion line will guide the ball's trajectory.

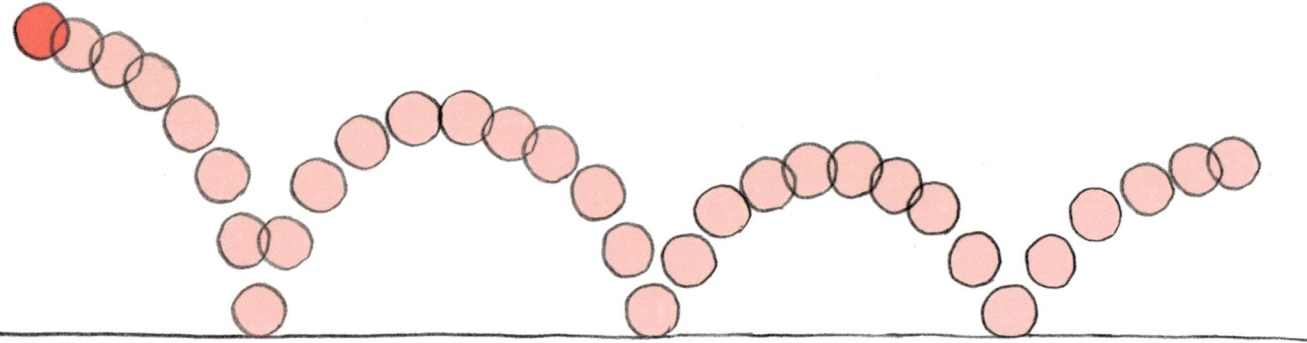

On the rest of the pages, draw a horizontal line across the page, and lightly mark the motion line. Then draw a circle on each page, changing its position slightly. Every circle follows the path of the motion line.

Make sure to draw the circles closer together at the top of the curves and more spaced out before and after they bounce. Erase the motion lines when you are done. Then test the animation and see the ball bouncing.

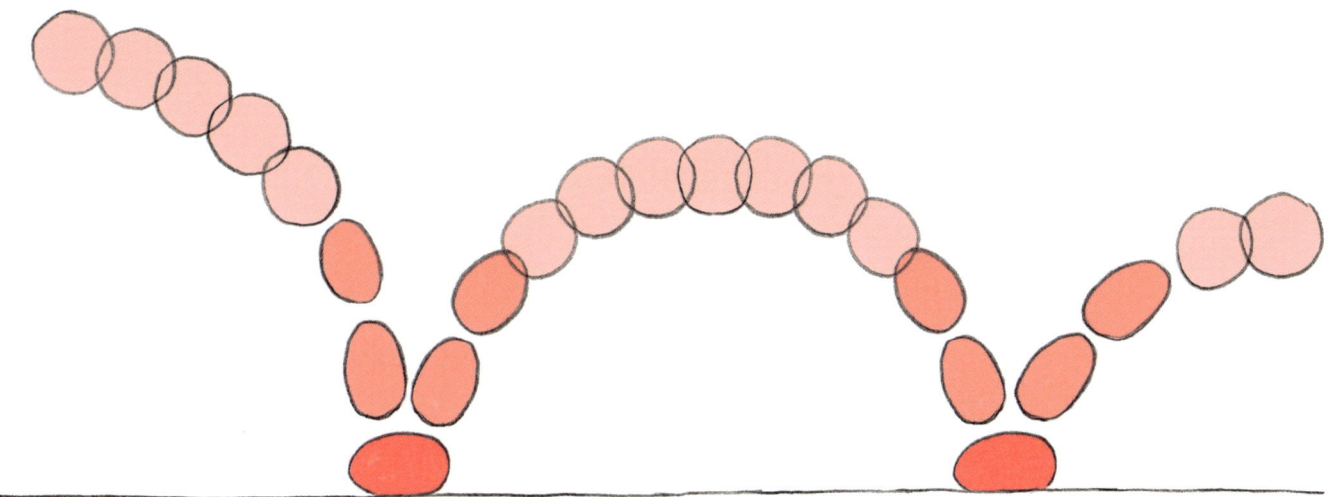

Imagine that the ball is elastic and changes its form every time it bounces. This time, use a flip book or notepad with 24 blank pages. Follow the same steps as in the previous exercise, but replace the bouncing circles with squashed, stretched ones. Test the animation, and see what happens. When you vary the form, the ball appears softer and more flexible.

Now do your own experiments. What would happen if you animated a heavier or lighter ball. How would the timing and spacing change?

TIP
The secret to mastering flip book timing is to test, test, test! Use spare flip books to try out different frame rates for animation sequences before creating your final animation.

TIMING

In flip book animation, the standard frame rate is 24 frames per second. Timing can vary slightly depending on how quickly a person flips the pages, but your final animation usually will turn out well using this frame rate. Before attempting to animate more challenging projects, you may want to test the timing of your flip book using simple keyframes.

Draw a picture similar to this one. You will work with three different examples, so trace this drawing on two more pages, or make a copy to save yourself some time.

Divide the previous picture into 23 spaces, and draw the skateboarder on each of them. Then trace every figure on 24 pages of your flip book. Draw 1 figure per page, moving from left to right. Now test the flip book, and see the character move at a steady pace.

A frame rate of 24 frames for 1 second of animation is known as "animating in 1s." In this next exercise, you will learn how to animate in "2s." A common technique that can save you a lot of work, "animating in 2s" means doubling up every drawing. You need 12 drawings for 1 second of animation.

Divide the empty picture of the skateboarder into 11 spaces, and draw the figure in each space. This time, repeat the drawing of every figure for 2 pages of the flip book until you've completed 24 pages. Now test your flip book. As you can see, the skateboarder still moves well, but the animation flickers a bit.

Divide the first picture into five spaces. Then trace the figures on six pages of your flip book. When you test the animation, you will notice that the skateboarder moves incredibly fast, taking just a fraction of a second to complete the movement. Notice how difficult it is to follow the action.

With flip book animation, there are no rules regarding frame rate. You are not restricted by the film strip's length as in video or digital animation.

Try the following exercise to see how your animation looks when you combine different frame rates in the same sequence.

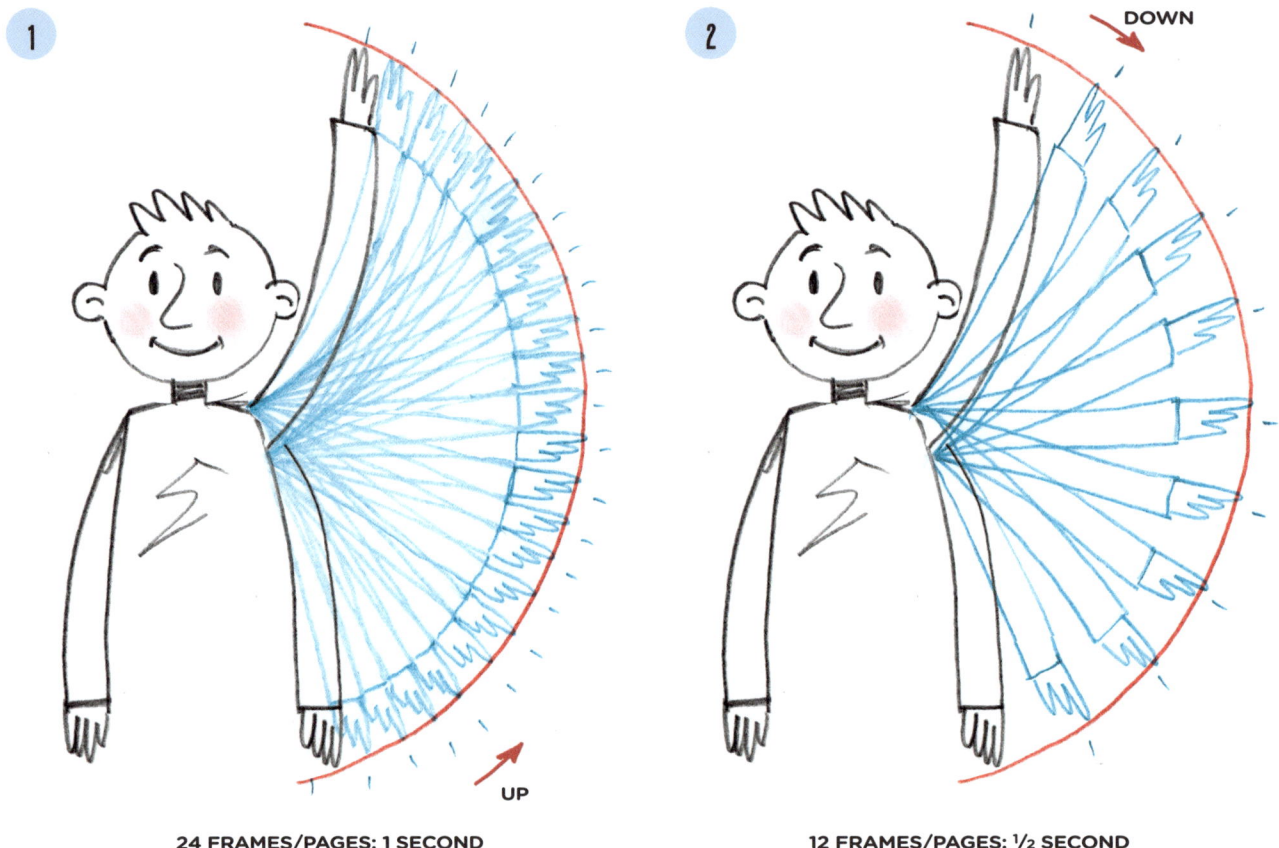

24 FRAMES/PAGES: 1 SECOND **12 FRAMES/PAGES: ½ SECOND**

The character is moving his arm up and down. In Figure 1, his arm starts in the down position and reaches the up position over 24 frames. As we mentioned earlier, the standard frame rate for 24 frames is 1 second.

In Figure 2, the character lowers his arm faster, taking only half a second to do it.

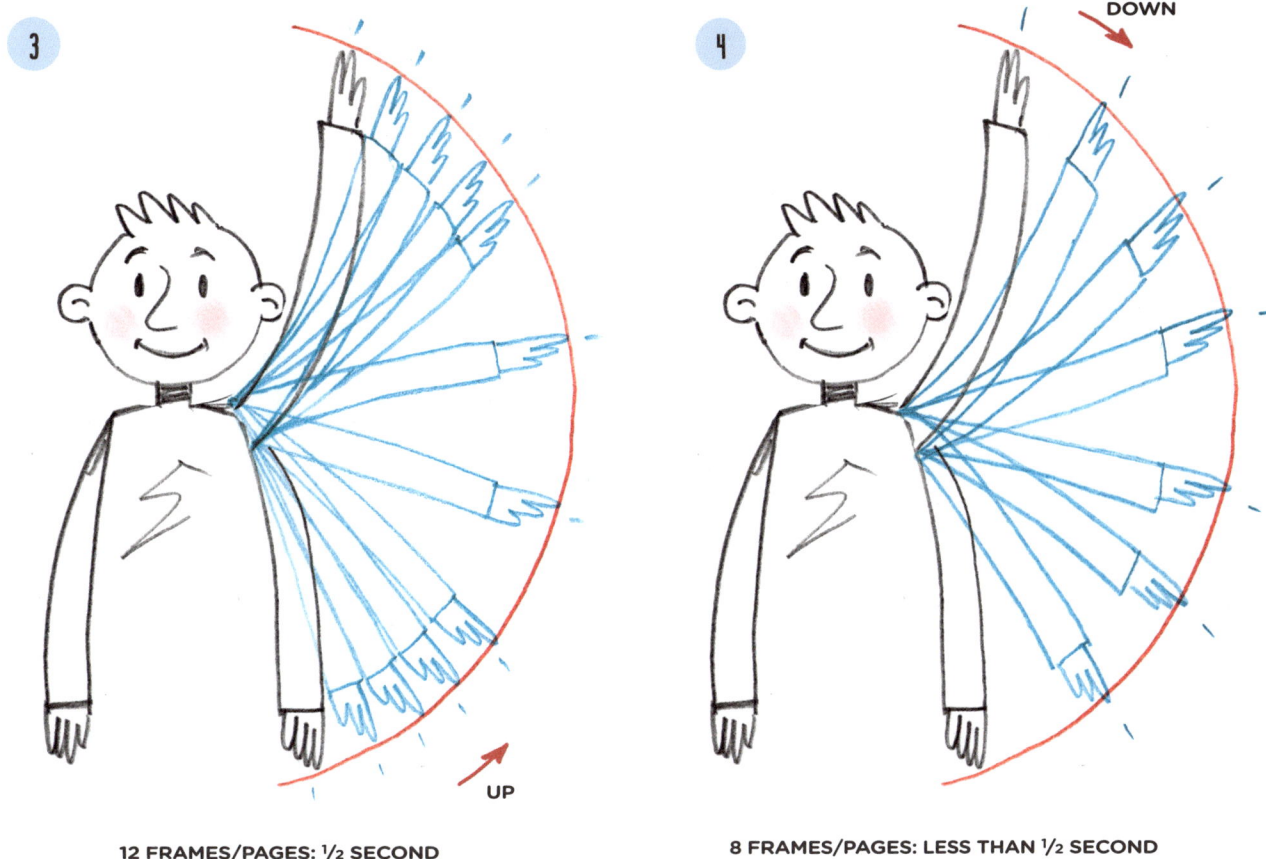

12 FRAMES/PAGES: ½ SECOND

8 FRAMES/PAGES: LESS THAN ½ SECOND

Figure 3 also takes half a second using some acceleration (see "Dynamics" on page 12).

Finally in Figure 4, he quickly moves his arm downward, taking less than half a second. To produce a pause between the different stages of this exercise, you can repeat the key poses (up and down) for 12 pages.

TIP
Never animate with a frame rate of less than 6 frames per second; this makes it difficult to perceive movement.

CHAPTER TWO

SIMPLE MOVEMENTS

KEYFRAMES AND INBETWEENS

In animation and filmmaking, keyframes, or extremes, serve as the defining points of an action. Inbetweens are the frames or drawings between two keyframes. Their purpose is to smooth the animation and produce the illusion of movement.

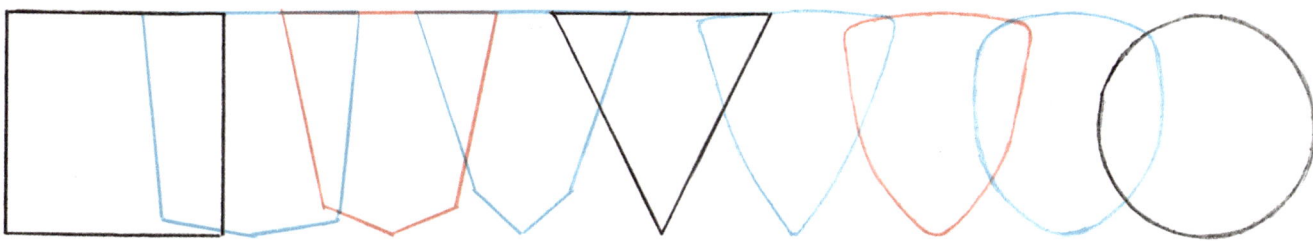

Morphing shapes can help you visualize the concept of keyframes and inbetweens. In the illustration above, the key drawings are the square, the triangle, and the circle. Making slight changes to the sides of those key geometrical shapes creates the inbetween drawings.

TIP
Vary the timing of an action by adding or subtracting inbetween drawings. Adding more in betweens can slow down and smooth out the motion.

This head turn is made using just two keyframes and two inbetweens. Even for a simple animation like this, guidelines help the animator align the head's shape with the rest of the character's features, such as his eyes, ears, and mouth.

YAWNING

To animate a character yawning, draw the keyframes, keeping in mind that it will take about 10 drawings to go from the first pose to the last. Then, using the keyframes as a guide, sketch a slightly different drawing for each inbetween. Finally, trace over the drawing in a flip book, and test it to make sure the timing works well.

A SKATEBOARDER'S JUMP

To animate a full pose-to-pose action like this skateboarder's jump, plan the movement in advance. Draw the keyframes and the ramp, and sketch the lines of action. Draw two lines for the head and two more for the skateboard.

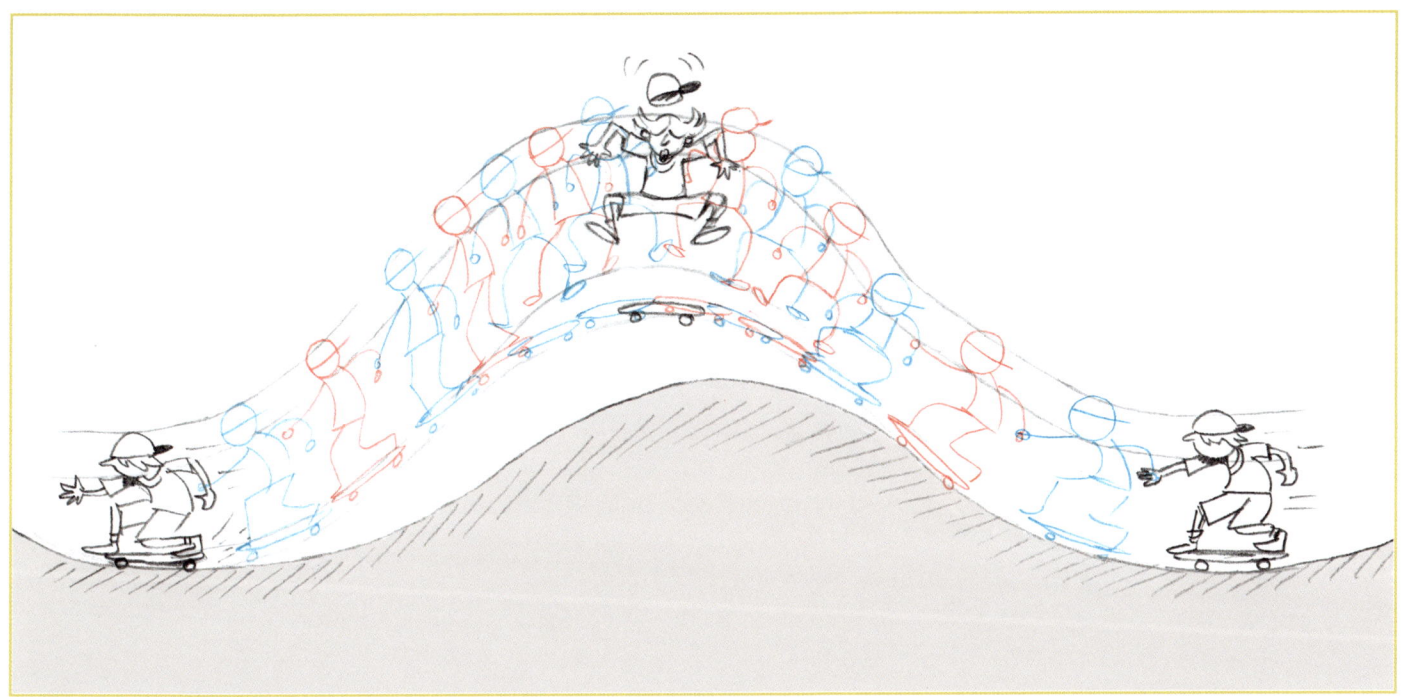

Draw the inbetweens. When the skateboarder is in the air, draw the inbetweens closer together to slow the action.

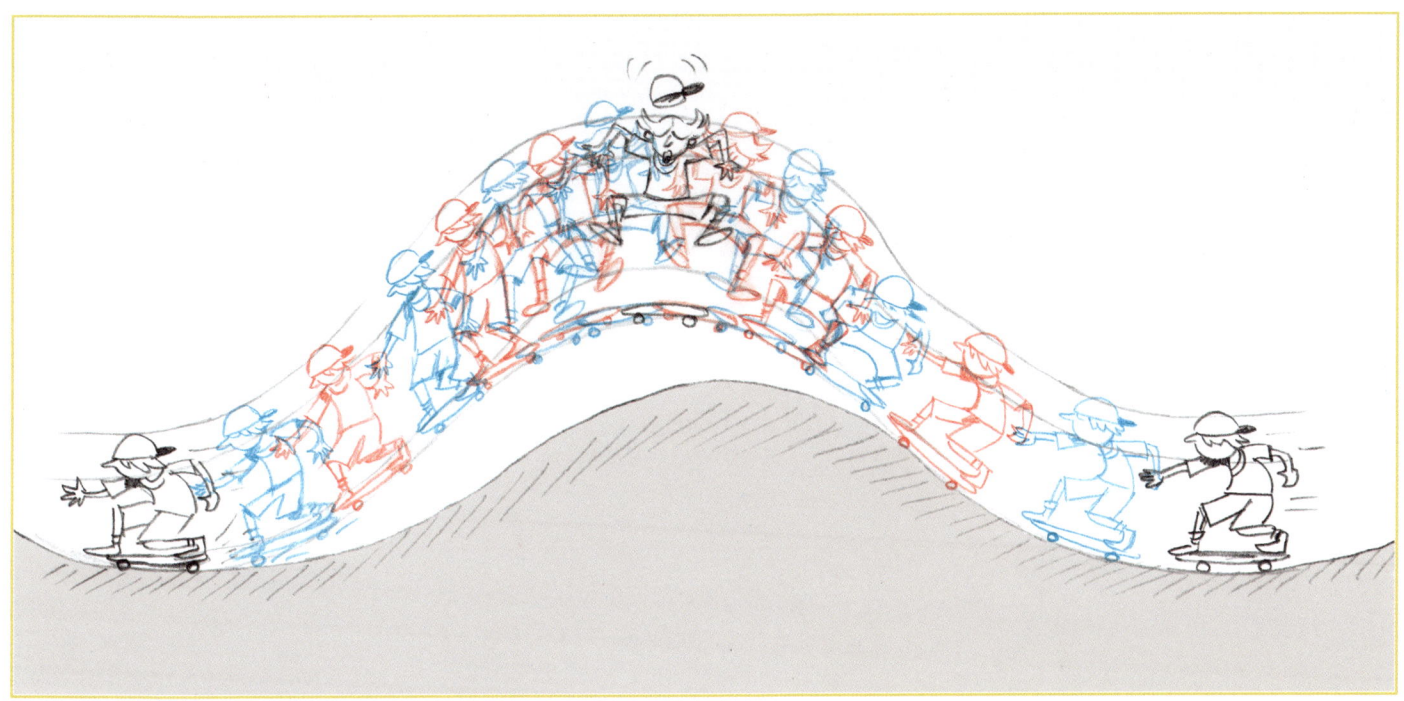

Transfer the basic form drawings to a flip book. I always test my drawings and check if the motions look accurate before adding details. I add or remove any inbetweens if the timing does not work well. Once you've tested the flip book, finish drawing the inbetweens, adding more details, and erase unnecessary lines.

TIP
Use basic shapes and colored pencils to sketch inbetween drawings for easier tracing later.

WALK CYCLES, RUN CYCLES, AND JUMPS

Begin with simple walk cycles, and then move on to running and jumping. Repeat the drawings as long as you'd like your characters to walk, run, or jump.

WALK CYCLES

One step consists of four drawings, shown below. Repeat these drawings on the other foot, and then draw the foot stepping again. Add inbetweens or animate the walk cycle in 2s (see page 17) to slow the monster's walking pace.

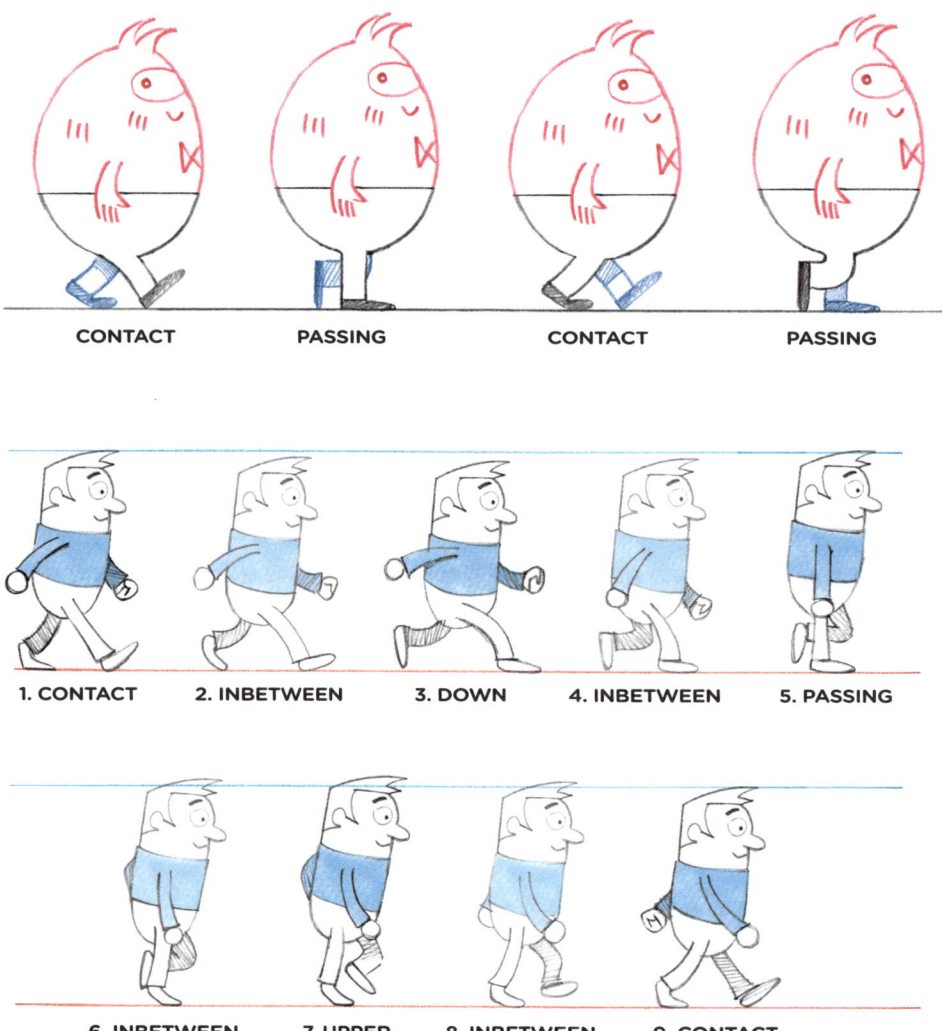

With this walk cycle, draw the two contact positions first. Then draw the down position, the passing position, and the upper position in that order. Finally, draw the inbetweens to smooth the animation and slow the pace.

Trace your drawings into a flip book, and test your animation. If everything looks good, clean up the drawings, and add some color. Place each drawing in the same spot on the page to have your character walk on the spot. To have your character walk cross the page, draw each image farther to the right. Make sure to space each drawing evenly for smooth action.

CONTACT   INBETWEEN   DOWN   INBETWEEN   PASSING   INBETWEEN   UPPER   INBETWEEN

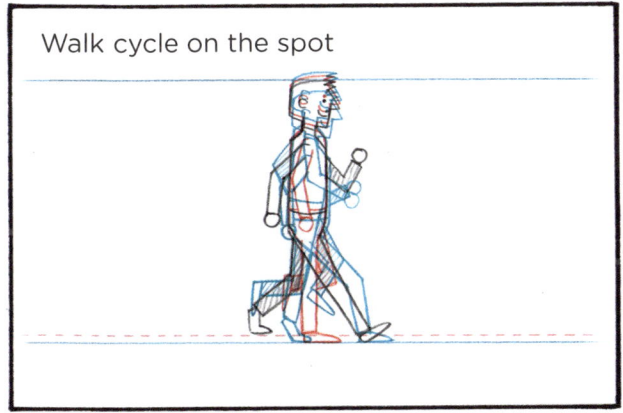

Walk cycle on the spot

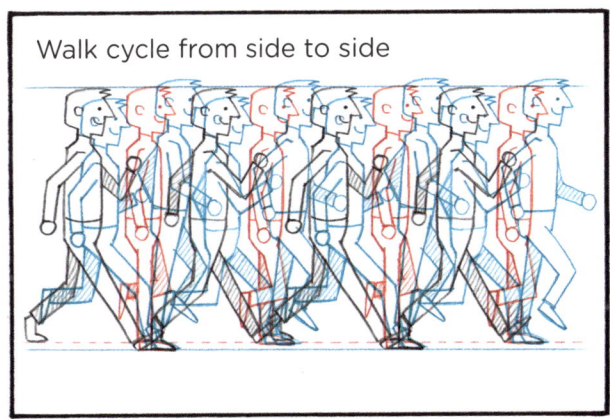

Walk cycle from side to side

RUN CYCLES

Run cycles share the same key poses as walk cycles. The main difference is that a run cycle includes a key pose after the upper position, when both feet are off the ground. Start by drawing the contact positions just like you did with the walk cycle. After the first contact pose, draw the down position. Then draw the passing position to define where your character's legs change direction. The next key drawing is the upper position; then draw a key pose in which both feet are off the ground. To finish the cycle, add one inbetween after the down and passing positions. Notice that a character's body moves higher when running than walking, so be careful not to draw the up and down poses too far from the reference line. Once you have drawn the walk or run cycle for a single step, you need to figure out the other leg's cycle.

TIP

Pay attention to the position of your character's head as it relates to the top reference line in your drawing. When the down position is at its lowest point, the upper position is at the highest and the passing position is just slightly over the reference line.

1. CONTACT
2. DOWN
3. INBETWEEN
4. PASSING
5. UPPER
6. OFF THE GROUND
7. CONTACT

JUMPS

A jump can start from a static position, or it can follow a walk or run. Wherever the jump starts, there must be an anticipation pose before the action can take place. This is when the body prepares itself to jump. Keep in mind that during an animated jump, a character's body reacts the same way as in the bouncing ball exercise on page 14: The body contracts before the jump and stretches during it. Before animating a jump, plan its trajectory and how much space it will require.

You can use lines of action to easily define the curve of a jump. Mark these following the lines of the character's head, waistline, knees, and feet. Then begin loosely tracing the different stages of the jump.

TIP

Before creating a walk cycle, run cycle, or jump, sketch your character on a piece of scratch paper, and use this as a guideline to trace over. This will keep the main features and proportions consistent.

ANTICIPATION

Anticipation prepares a viewer for an action. You can observe anticipation in many real-life situations, especially in sports. For example, think about the movement a pitcher makes before throwing a baseball. In cartoons, anticipation is used before almost every action, from jumps and throws to the subtle movement of a character's head before raising it.

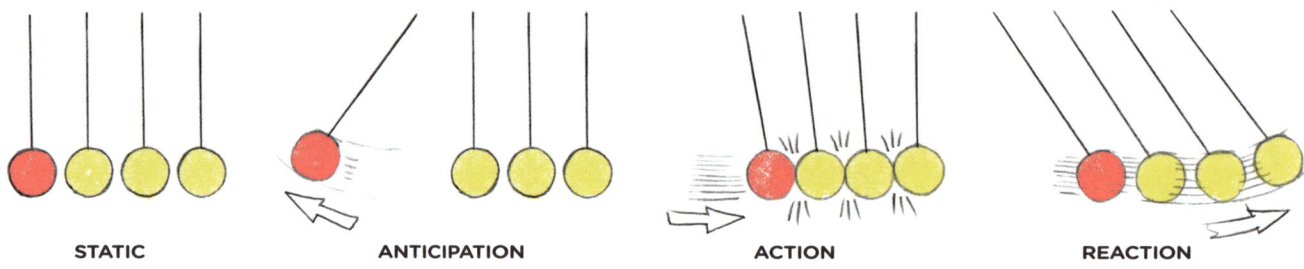

In this example, the red sphere retracts to the left, pushing the yellow spheres to the right. This demonstrates one of this principle's key points: The anticipation position and trajectory of an action should always go in opposite directions.

Before a superhero takes flight, he needs to prepare himself. When anticipation is applied to a cartoon character, the figure must be squashed and stretched, just like we did with the bouncing ball on page 15. Notice how the superhero moves down in the anticipation position because he will eventually go up.

BIRTHDAY BOY

This exercise will show you how anticipation works. Feel free to reproduce the whole action in your flip book or notepad, or just practice the anticipation and action parts.

This couple is celebrating the man's birthday. Repeat this drawing on 12 pages to establish the scene.

The male character leans backward and prepares to take a big deep breath before...

...blowing out the candles ... and the cake as well. Repeat this drawing on three pages, moving the cake slightly closer to the woman's face on each page.

The cake is all over the woman's face. The man looks worried, while the woman remains static. Repeat this drawing on six pages.

The man turns around to run away, and the woman gets ready to jump over the table to chase him.

The woman jumps over the table while the man leaves the scene.

The man disappears. Complete the woman's jump on the last pages of your flip book.

CHAPTER THREE

CHARACTER DESIGN

YOUR ARTISTIC FREEDOM

Designing characters is one of the most fun and rewarding parts of the animation process. You have endless creative possibilities and the artistic freedom to make your characters look and act in any way you can imagine.

The easiest way to designing characters is by using simple shapes, such as lines (straight and curved) and other geometric forms. To create full-body characters, I usually start with a circle or an ellipse for the head. Then I draw a line, which can be curved or straight, for the spine. Notice how much the characters' appearances change when I vary their shapes and sizes and the lengths of their spines.

TIP
Before working in your final character design, doodle some ideas, such as body shapes, faces, and clothes. Try not to add too many details for now. The goal is to familiarize yourself with the characters and determine which features will work better later on.

FAMILY FUN

In this exercise, you will draw the members of a family beginning with circles, ellipses, and lines. By stretching and squashing these shapes, you can define the characters' heights, ages, and styles.

1

Draw each character using basic shapes and lines.

2

Add facial features and hair. Then create the contours of the characters' bodies. You can vary the volumes of their bodies and their limbs.

3

Refine your drawing by adding details. Then remove the guidelines and add hatching and shading to create volume and make your drawing look more interesting.

PIRATE'S BOOTY

The goal of this exercise is to convey the personality of each character using body structure. You will draw a small group of pirates: an evil little captain, a bearded pirate, a good-natured cabin boy, and a silly giant. Remember that it's often a good idea to exaggerate the characters' proportions so they look more interesting and funny when animated.

1

Start by sketching some ovals and circles, but stretch and squash them. Also play with the scale of the characters. Notice that the giant pirate's elbows feature circles that are considerably bigger than the other characters' to represent his size. Draw a distended line for his spine to illustrate his large belly. Some of the pirates are going to be holding props, so sketch shapes that will become swords, a bucket, the captain's hook, and the captain's wooden leg. The captain's parrot flies over his head.

2

If necessary, do some research to find out what a pirate captain's hat and the other objects look like. Then draw the bodies, facial features, clothes, and props.

3

To finish the design, add details, like a skull and crossbones on the captain's hat, and refine the hair, beard, clothes, and props for each character. Add some hatching lines, and finish drawing the parrot.

MONSTER MASH

Here you will create a bunch of random creatures with different body shapes and structures, such as a small vampire mouse, a flying creature, an old-fashioned robot, and a big monster. Each character features a very different body shape and size.

1 Draw the vampire mouse using circles, ellipses, and lines. For the others, use the same shapes as well as semicircles, rectangles, and irregular forms like the one for the big monster. As in the previous exercise, draw lines for the arms and circles and ellipses to distinguish the hands, feet, and joints.

2 Add eyes to your characters, and define the contours of their bodies, their arms, and their legs. The big monster doesn't need legs, so you can sketch some zigzag lines instead. Also define the vampire mouse's clothes.

3 Add details, and erase the guidelines you no longer need. Add hatching to create volume, shadows, and details, and fill in other areas with a colored pencil.

TIP

Experiment and sketch many variations before beginning the final character design. Almost any shape can become a character when you draw eyes, mouths, or arms on it, so keep trying until you're happy with the characters you've drawn.

FACIAL EXPRESSIONS

Here are guidelines for a few of the most common emotions and reactions. Notice that the outlines of the boy's head and nose remain the same, and only his eyes, eyebrows, and mouth change. Notice how the shape of the girl's face varies as she changes her facial expressions. Exaggeration can effectively convey emotions too.

HAPPINESS LAUGHTER

SURPRISE ANGER

HAPPINESS LAUGHTER

SURPRISE ANGER

Animators will often stand in front of a mirror and study their facial expressions and body language that convey a particular emotion. Try it! You can also watch some classic or dramatic films to observe the actors. Do some quick sketches to capture the movements, feelings, and emotions.

Body language is often essential for communicating an emotion. Notice how the position of the character's arms, legs, tail, and ears change in each expression.

ANIMATING A FACE

Practice drawing facial expressions and familiarize yourself with timing animations in a flip book. Grab a notebook, pencils, and colored pencils in case you want to add some color!

1

Trace this picture on 5 sheets of paper. Then draw 2 inbetweens.

2

Trace this picture on 5 sheets of paper. Then draw 1 inbetween.

3

Trace this picture on 5 sheets of paper. Then draw 3 inbetweens.

4

Trace this picture on 5 sheets of paper. Then draw 2 inbetweens, and make the tears disappear gradually.

5

Trace this picture on 5 sheets of paper. You don't need to do any inbetween drawings this time.

6

Trace this picture on 5 sheets of paper.

CHAPTER FOUR

WRITING A STORY

KEEPING IT SIMPLE

You can think of flip books like short, simple jokes: They take only a few seconds to tell. The flip book animator's challenge, is to create a very short animated story using conventional storytelling methods. Experiment with animating a sports sequence, a familiar event, or a Wild West gunfight. The possibilities are endless; you just need to come up with an idea!

1 Define the characters.
Who are your characters? Is there only one, or are there several? Loosely sketch your characters before fully designing them. Determine their personalities, moods, body features, and roles in the story. A flip book needs pretty simple characters, so try playing with some common types.

2 Choose the location.
Another important aspect to consider: where the story will be located. With flip book animation, the background must be drawn on each page, so keep it as simple as possible.

3 What's the problem?
Flip books are short, but their plots are constructed the same way as in any longer story. That means your story needs a beginning, a middle, and an ending or a resolution. To begin the story, set up a problem, goal, or catalyst to the problem or goal. Then you'll need to decide what happens in the middle and how the story unfolds to its climax.

4 The resolution
The last step in a story is the resolution or ending. Is the problem or goal accomplished by the end? What is the punch line or twist in the story?

STORYBOARDING

Once you've chosen the characters, setting, and plot for your flip book, it's time to storyboard. Storyboards look like comic strips, with panels where you can identify every action and camera angle that will appear in an animation.

STAGING

Pay attention to the staging of your characters. Consider the subjects' proportions, and leave enough space in each frame for the necessary actions to occur. Remember to place the characters clearly in the scene to make them the center of attention.

MAPPING OUT THE PLOT

The following story has a very simple plot. There are only two characters, a boy and his dog, and the action is set outside. While playing with a bubble wand set, the boy blows a bubble that gets bigger and bigger until it explodes, covering both characters in soap. Here is the storyboard.

1 Title: "The Big Bubble Bang." This frame doesn't need animation.

2 The boy blows a bubble. The bubble gets bigger. The dog looks at the boy.

3 The boy continues blowing the bubble, but now he's blowing harder. The dog looks fearfully at him.

4 The boy has finished and looks tired. The dog is afraid of what is about to happen.

5 The bubble explodes. Bang!

6 The boy and the dog are covered in soap. Ending titles: "The End!"

ANIMATING A FLYING SUPERHERO

Now that you've learned the basics of animation, you are ready to put them into practice with this fun exercise. The plot for this flip book is very simple: A flying superhero is attacked by his archenemy and gets transformed into … a giant roasted chicken!

CHARACTER DESIGN

 1

Use simple shapes to sketch the superhero, and then refine the lines and add details.

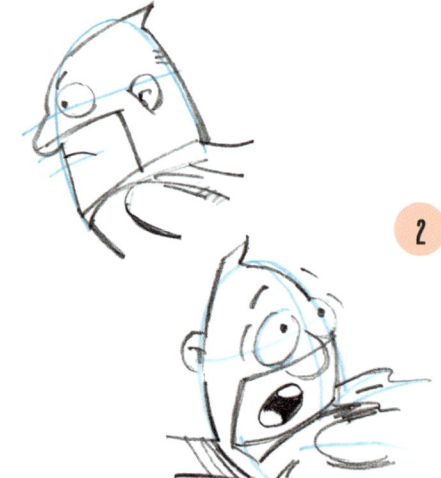

2 Sketch a few of his facial expressions. These will help you later.

 3

Sketch the superhero's archenemy in his flying saucer using simple shapes. The archenemy always has an angry frown on his face, and his pose remains the same, so you don't need to draw different expressions or views of this character.

4 Add color.

STORYBOARD

This story has just four steps.

1. Introduce your superhero as he flies through the sky.

2. His archenemy, Alien Chicken, surprises him.

3. The superhero is zapped with a laser.

4. The superhero is transformed into a flying roasted chicken.

BACKGROUND
Your background will be four times the width of the flip book.

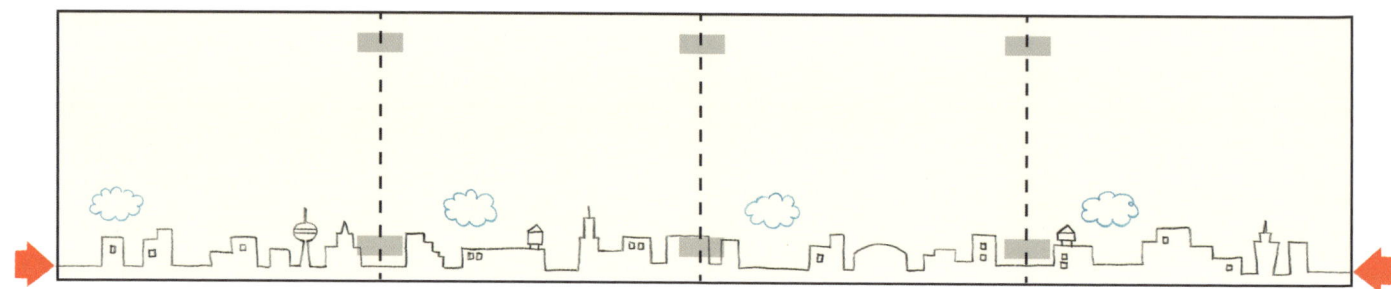

Using a light box, trace the background, moving it slightly to the left on each new page so it looks like the characters are flying over the city. Make sure both ends of the background can be joined.

LINES OF ACTION
Sketch the characters' actions using basic shapes before animating. Don't worry about being too precise; use colored pencils to draw the steps and to mark the lines of action. You'll trace over this rough layout when you draw the final keyframes and inbetweens.

TIP

Once you have finished the keyframes, do a quick test of the flip book to check if it works well. Before moving to the next stage, make any necessary changes if you find something wrong with the movement or timing.

KEYFRAMES

Now it's time to work in the final animation. You'll start by drawing the keyframes on the pages where you previously traced the background. You are going to animate this flip book in fours over 64 pages, distributed like this: 16 pages for the intro, 8 pages for each of the 4 key actions, and 16 pages for the outro. Draw keyframes using these annotations as a reference.

1. Animate the motion lines and the cape slightly from page 1 to page 16.

2. Draw this keyframe on page 24 of your flip book. Remember that you will do the inbetweens later.

3. Draw this keyframe on page 32.

4. Draw this keyframe on page 40.

5. Alien Chicken will have disappeared completely by page 48.

6. Animate the motion lines and the chicken wings slightly over the last 16 pages.

INBETWEENS

The final part of the animation process is to draw the inbetweens. The superhero will morph into a chicken between pages 32 and 48.

TIP
Draw lightly first. You can use a blue pencil in case you have to erase something or make any changes.

Do one more test of the animation, and add color!

DR. JEKYLL AND MR. HYDE

The main character is Dr. Jekyll, a thin, nerdy professor who drinks a potion that turns him into Mr. Hyde, a muscular, good-looking beachgoer. Use basic shapes to create your characters. Then add other features, details, and colors to the characters.

The story begins in a laboratory, where Dr. Jekyll is drinking a potion. Then comes a transformation sequence, lasting for a few seconds, that is animated using the straight-ahead method (which means animating frame by frame until the sequence is complete), after which Mr. Hyde is revealed in a new location. A title sequence will go at the beginning and end of this 64-page flip book. The keyframes are listed here.

① Opening title: "Dr. Jekyll." Repeat this picture for 6 pages.

② Dr. Jekyll is in his lab. He sees a jar containing a magical potion on the table and grabs it. Draw this scene over 6 pages. On the last 2 pages, Dr. Jekyll moves his hand and grabs the jar. He holds the jar and looks at it. Repeat this drawing for 6 pages.

③ Dr. Jekyll leans his head back to gulp down the magical potion. Draw this action over 2 pages.

4 Repeat the following drawing for 4 pages: Dr. Jekyll holds the empty jar and feels great until he discovers that ...

5 ... something is wrong. Draw this for 2 pages.

6 Cut to extreme close-up. Repeat over 2 pages.

7 Cut to a more extreme close-up. This is the first frame using the straight-ahead method. Experiment and have fun here. Move the different elements around, and add special effects. Draw this scene over 12 pages until the scene in which Mr. Hyde's face is revealed.

8 Dr. Jekyll's features morph before distorting into Mr. Hyde's.

9 Mr. Hyde's face is revealed.

10 Cut from an extreme close-up to a close-up. Repeat this picture over 2 pages.

11 Mr. Hyde is delighted with his new appearance. Repeat this picture for 2 pages.

12 Cut to a long shot of a beach with Mr. Hyde in the center and people wearing bathing suits in the background. Draw this scene over 6 pages.

13 Mr. Hyde flexes his muscles, and the people in the background cheer for him. Draw the action on 2 pages, and repeat the last keyframe over the next 4 pages.

14 Closing title: "& Mr. Hyde." Repeat this drawing over 6 pages.

CHAPTER FIVE

TAKING IT TO THE NEXT LEVEL

ANIMATING DANCERS

Animating dancers is fun, and the results are often pretty amazing. This exercise will teach you about weight, rhythm, and how the body moves and turns. When animating a flip book, you don't need to worry about tempo or timing your animation to go with music. Just focus on simple dancing routines.

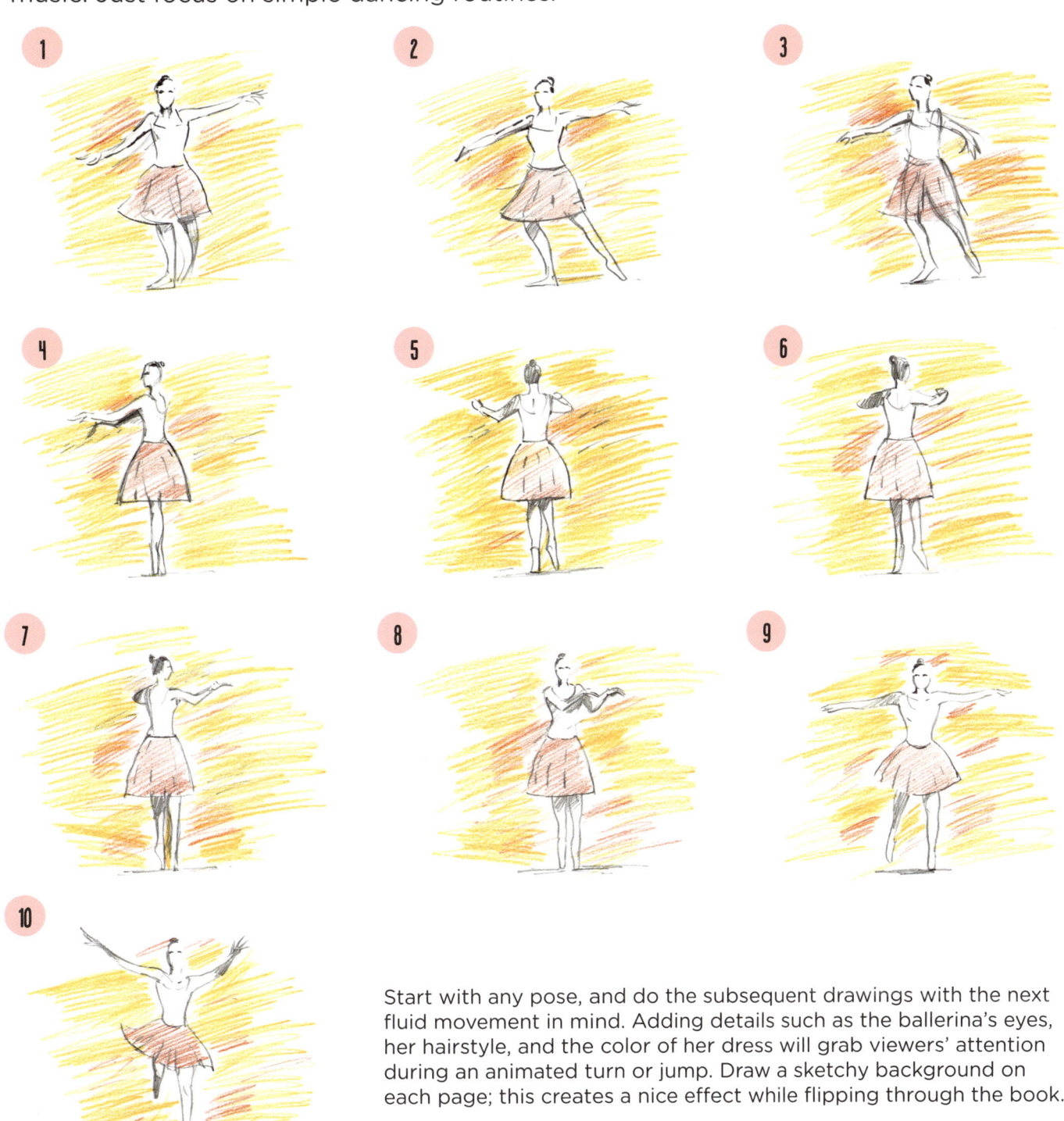

Start with any pose, and do the subsequent drawings with the next fluid movement in mind. Adding details such as the ballerina's eyes, her hairstyle, and the color of her dress will grab viewers' attention during an animated turn or jump. Draw a sketchy background on each page; this creates a nice effect while flipping through the book.

You can simplify the ballerina figure or even leave her off of some of the pages. Add new colors and, if working in pencil, smudge some areas to create the effect of movement. Periodically test your flip book throughout the animation process. Get rid of any drawings that don't flow well.

ANIMATING ANIMALS

Before you start animating animals, it is important to understand their anatomy. Four-legged animals are drawn using basic geometric shapes and varied line lengths to represent their bones. To create the shape of a cat or dog, draw two circles for its body and an ellipse for the head. Then mark lines for the bone structure, and draw small ellipses for the toes.

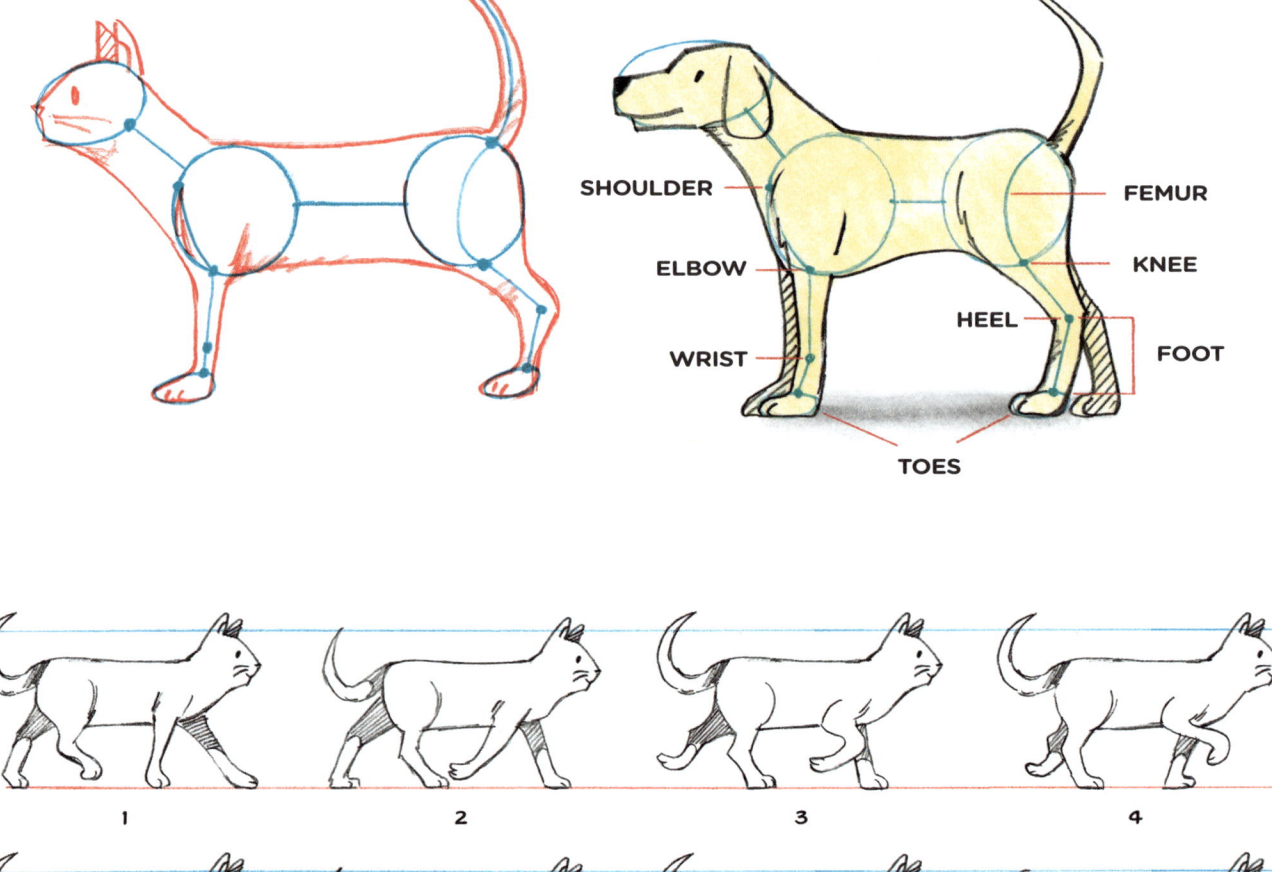

All four-legged animals walk similarly. Animal walk cycles can be tricky to animate, because there are two pairs of legs moving at the same time.

The easiest way to draw a bird is by marking its body structure with circles for the head and body. Then outline the body of the bird. When animating avian characters, imagine the wings as arms and the tips of the feathers as fingers.

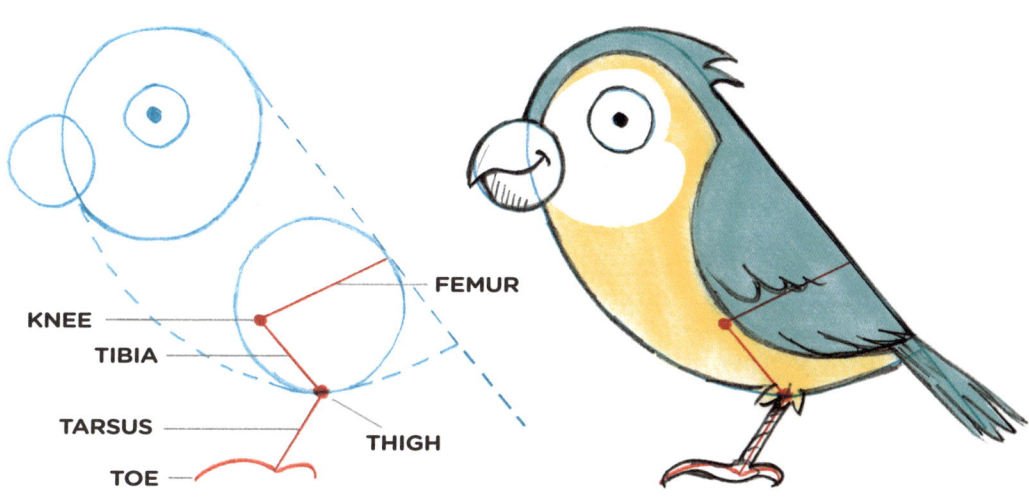

In this flying cycle, you can see the full movement of a bird's wings.

BINDING A FLIP BOOK

You can use this simple method for binding your flip books, whether you do your animations on individual pieces of paper or plan to animate your book later on.

 1

Ask an adult to cut all of your paper to the same size with a utility knife and cutting mat. Clip all of the pages together with binder clips placed at the top of the book. Check that the spine looks perfectly even, or use a scrap of sandpaper to even it out.

 2

Use a paintbrush to apply glue to the book's spine. Clean off any excess glue with a piece of old fabric. Let the glue dry, and apply a second coat. Place a weight on top of your flip book, and let it rest for an hour.

3

Measure the sides and spine of the flip book, and fold a sheet of card stock to create a front and back cover for your book. Place a sheet of paper over the inside front and back covers, and apply glue to the spine. Wait five minutes, and then apply another layer.

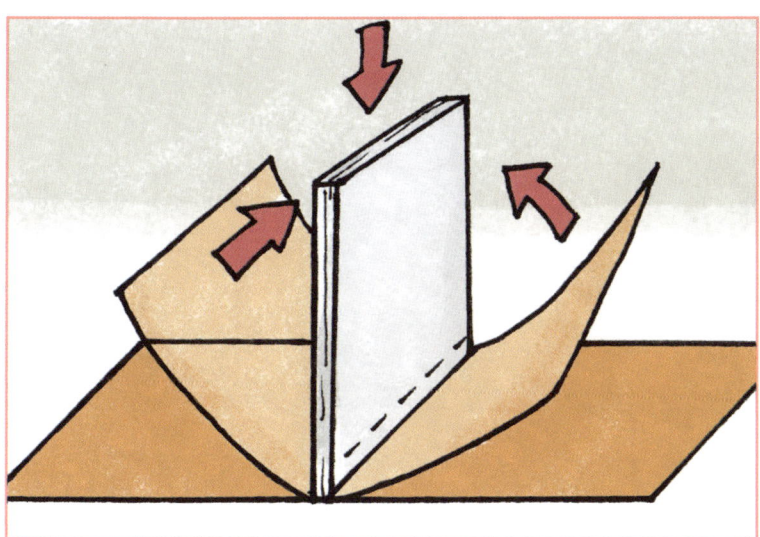

4

Place the spine of the flip book over the glue, and press down firmly. Fold the cover's sides, and place a weight on top of the entire flip book. Let it rest for a few hours.

5

Your flip book is now bound and ready! Test the pages to make sure your book flips well.

ABOUT THE AUTHOR

David Hurtado was born in Spain and graduated with a degree in animation from the Norwich University of the Arts in the United Kingdom. He worked as a graphic designer before starting his career as a freelance illustrator and animator. David has created illustrations for many leading publishing companies, as well as heritage projects and advertisements. In the animation field, he has collaborated on several short films, worked on animated ads for TV and produced animations for the educational field. In his free time, David enjoys drawing comics, watching films and spending time outdoors, preferably at the beach. Learn more about David at davidhurtado.com.